I0197871

F. A. Gore Ouseley, Edwin George Monk

Unison Chants for the Psalter

A Collection of Single Anglican Changs Appropriated to the Daily Psalms

F. A. Gore Ouseley, Edwin George Monk

Unison Chants for the Psalter
A Collection of Single Anglican Changs Appropriated to the Daily Psalms

ISBN/EAN: 9783337296896

Printed in Europe, USA, Canada, Australia, Japan

Cover: Foto ©Lupo / pixelio.de

More available books at **www.hansebooks.com**

FOR

THE PSALTER

A COLLECTION OF

Single Anglican Chants

APPROPRIATED TO THE DAILY PSALMS IN THE BOOK OF COMMON PRAYER

EXPRESSLY SELECTED AND ADAPTED FOR THE

USE OF CHURCH CHOIRS AND CONGREGATIONS

EDITED BY

The Rev. CANON SIR F. A. G. OUSELEY

BART., M.A., MUS. DOC., PRECENTOR OF HEREFORD, AND PROFESSOR OF MUSIC IN THE UNIVERSITY OF OXFORD, 1855-89

AND

EDWIN GEORGE MONK

MUS. DOC., OXON., ORGANIST AND MASTER OF THE CHOIR, YORK MINSTER, 1859-83.

ORGAN HARMONIES.
PRICE FIVE SHILLINGS.

LONDON & NEW YORK
NOVELLO, EWER AND CO.
OXFORD: JAMES PARKER AND CO.

THE VOICE PART, PRICE ONE SHILLING.

PREFACE.

It were much to be wished that Chanting of the Psalter could be lifted into like favour in our Churches with Hymn-singing; this being well-nigh universal, the former but very partial. Only a small proportion of each Congregation is found to take part in chanting the daily Psalms, while Hymns are commonly sung (or attempted) by nearly every one; and this in spite of that strain upon the vocal compass too often involved in the practice. It is true that the fixed value of every note in these tunes (together with their brevity and unvarying rhythm, as well as symmetrical structure), presents the simplest of all forms for making Church Music practicable and popular with congregations; yet the Single Anglican Chant is still shorter and simpler; while its chief difficulty, arising from the mixture of Recitative with Rhythm, constitutes its very life and charm.

On the claims and preciousness of the Psalter, in this connection, as the inalienable heritage of the Catholic Church of all time, it is needless to enlarge: the paramount value and richness of these divinely-inspired "Psalms, Hymns, and Spiritual Songs," being widely felt and acknowledged among Churchmen.*

In furtherance of a more general chanting of the Psalter in Churches, the present Work is an attempt to supply a plan sufficiently easy to secure extensive adoption, yet varied enough to be attractive, upon the one and only basis regarded by the Editors as being universally practicable—viz., the employment of Single Chant Melodies, to be sung "in Unison."

So largely of late years have love of Church Music and skill therein grown and spread among us, that no argument seems necessary to recommend Chanting rather than mere *reading* of the Psalter. Assuming this, a few words will suffice to explain the rationale of the present fresh effort to facilitate and promote so inspiring and devout an exercise in Choirs and Congregations.

In order that each daily portion of the Psalms should be sung without fatigue, and the Chanting be hearty and impressive, it should always be "Antiphonal," *i.e.*, responsive from side to side, north to south, "Decani to Cantoris:"† a method which, while perhaps suggested in Old Testament history,‡ is in full accordance with the primitive practice of Catholic Christendom; as that is with the tradition of St. Ignatius, who in a vision heard Angels so singing.§ This

---

* " Profitable beyond words as is the instruction conveyed to us in every word of Scripture, yet the Psalms have been the most directly and visibly useful part of the whole volume, having been the prayer-book of the Church ever since they were written; and have done more (as far as we dare judge) to prepare souls for heaven, than any of the inspired books, except the Gospels."— *Dr. J. H. Newman; Sermon 1, Vol.* 11.
   Bishop Alexander, in his Bampton Lectures, says: " Our Cathedrals are so many shrines for the Psalter." Why not, also, our Parish Churches and Chapels?

   † A relic of this ancient " use" still survives in the common practice of alternate verse reading, between Minister and People. It may be added that in large Choral gatherings it has sometimes been found advantageous to divide the assembled Singers into two bodies, Nave and Chancel, as an exceptional alternative to the usual plan. In Unison Chanting it is also effective sometimes to divide the verses between the high voices of women and children and the low voices of men.

   ‡ Exodus xv., ver. 20, 21; Isaiah vi., ver. 3.

   § " Singing alternately, as the custom of God's Church on earth has been from at least the days of the Temple to the present time."—*Rev. J. H. Blunt's Annotated Bible.*

obviously involves *division* of the voices into two bodies or sides; a necessity usually fatal to well sustained *part*-singing in small Choirs; while often in moderate-sized ones only a feeble handful of voices is left on each side to take up its verse, or half-verse, with requisite promptness, animation, and vigour. It may fairly be held that sixteen Choristers—eight on each side, two to each part—is nearly, if not quite, the smallest number capable of forming an effective *four-part Chorus*. In the rare cases of country, or even town Churches, where such a body exists, no small degree of *cultivation* of voice and method are essential for the attainment of good results where the ordinary Single or Double Chants in vogue are used. Yet further, it may be safely asserted, that if faultless chanting can be anywhere found in union with the "over-tuneful and discursive phrases, and immoderately high and low Reciting-Notes" too common in such Chants, it can only be in Cathedrals, College-Chapels, and a few important and well endowed Churches, where, with picked voices, subject to diligent practice and teaching, the Psalms are daily sung at Matins and Evensong throughout the year.

If this be so, *how* then is the Psalter to be chanted in that vast majority of Churches which have only *small* Choirs, with rugged voices, and little training?

The Editors' answer is ready, and unfaltering:—Let it be sung in Vocal Unison; supported, emphasized, and coloured by *Instrumental Harmony*, if possible on an *Organ*. In this way, even with few voices, under proper teaching and discipline—(especially in the case of children, as to securing good and fluent *reading*, before chanting the words is attempted)—a happy result may sooner or later be obtained, provided that the melodies employed be simple, solid, so far as may be, attractive, and, above all, of *general practicability*.

The present Work, projected (and even announced) some score of years ago, is intended to meet the need indicated, by providing a Series of easy and suitable Chants, *for Unison Singing only*, for the monthly course of the Psalter in the Book of Common Prayer. Not only have small and moderately qualified Choirs been kept in view, but also particularly the *Voice of the great Congregation*. In order to secure this much to be desired end—Chanting of the Daily Psalms by Choir and Congregation combined—the following means are proposed :—

    I. *Singing in Unison* (strictly speaking, *Octave*-Singing).

    II. Employment of Chants of *Restricted Compass* only; especially as to all Reciting-Notes. [No note lower than $\flat$ or higher than $\flat$ is employed for *Recitations*: these extremes being avoided as far as possible; the former occurring mostly when a subdued, the latter when a jubilant note is required. The *Melodies* never extend below or above ; such outside limits being very occasionally used, and then only for short Psalms, or portions of Psalms.]

III. Provision for *Change of Chant* at every fresh Psalm; and also, whenever in the course
      of any of the longer Psalms, such change could be made to follow the significance
      of the Sacred Text, conduce to its clearer understanding, or enforce its teaching.

IV.   Suggestion for occasional *Change of Instrumental Harmony* as a further mode (often of
      much value and potency) of heightening the desired expression; or of calling
      attention to important divisions, and changes of subject or utterance, in cases
      when actual change of the voice-part seemed undesirable.

The Editors still maintain their old convictions as to the superiority of Single Anglican
Chants over all other forms;* not only on the ground of their greater simplicity and liveliness,†
but also, particularly, for the ease with which they can be employed at *any* verse of the Psalm,
whenever a change of Chant is desired; and for any *grouping* whatever of verses—an advantage
not belonging to Double Chants—which, on the contrary, often cause resort to the "clumsy
expedient" of the "half-chant," for the cure of inseparable redundancy. Once admit longer
forms, and Triple or Quadruple must logically follow the introduction of Double Chants; and
thus, putting aside other objections to their use, we should certainly be admitting *a serious obstacle
to Congregational* Chanting of the Psalter.

This Collection therefore consists of Single Chants only. Its contents, as well as their
apportionment to the Psalms, are largely based upon "*The Psalter with Chants,*" 1879, of the
Editors, and "*The Anglican Chant Book,*" 1880; but these sources have been added to and
enriched, by permitted quotations from various standard Collections, as well as by numerous
original contributions from friendly pens. Indispensable restrictions, both as to compass and
character of the Chants, their association in easy and natural sequence for each daily portion of
the Psalms, and fitting combination therewith throughout the monthly course, have narrowed the
Editors' choice, as well as excluded a few well-known specimens; but such difficulties were
inherent in their undertaking, and call for no further comment.

Transposition has been largely resorted to, in order to meet the requirements of a limited
vocal range; and, more rarely, slight modifications and excisions have been necessary, to carry
through and ensure the specific scope and purpose of the Work. As to Transposition the Editors
keenly feel all the arguments that may be urged against it. Yet, on the other hand—for such a
purpose as the present—those in its favour seem still weightier. This Work, indeed, could not have
been undertaken with any prospect of extensive usefulness without its unsparing employment.

It will not, it is hoped, be imagined by any that in this advocacy of Unisonal Chanting
distinctively for the Psalter there is the slightest wish to discourage the use of Choral *Harmony* in
Divine Worship, with all the moving and noble effects produced by well-balanced and refined

---

* "Chants are either Single or Double. The latter admit of the most variety; yet it may be doubted whether they are in any
other respect preferable to Single Chants, which were first invented."—*Preface to Dr. Crotch's Collection of Single and Double
Chants.*

† "It might be supposed that Single Chants would prove tiresome from their being repeated so often, but, on the contrary,
their very brevity appears to make them the more animated."—*Preface to 1st Edition of "The Anglican Chant Book."*—1850.

Part-Singing; or a desire for the further extension of Unison-Singing; beyond its common
employment for the *People's Part* in Confession, Lord's Prayer, Response, and Creed.
Not to mention simple "Anthems" and "Services," which are available for Choirs where
practice and discipline prevail, the Canticles with carefully selected Chants, as well as Hymn-
Tunes, may readily be sung in Harmony by such Choirs against the Congregational Unison,
by reason of constant recurrence, and consequent familiarity: advantages which cannot
attach to the Hundred and Fifty Psalms of David, which do not quickly become well known to
those singers who chant on Sundays only, and are unaccustomed to *daily* use of the Psalter in
Matins and Evensong.

To the best of the Editors' belief there is no Book extant which provides a full and com-
plete scheme of Anglican Chants adapted for Unison-Singing, and appropriated to the entire
Psalter upon the plan they now put forward. For that large proportion of English Churchmen
who are not only satisfied with Chants of national growth, but enjoy them, love them, and find
in them the most natural and expressive vehicle for singing the Psalter in their mother-tongue,
it is believed that the thought and labour which have been devoted to the preparation of this
monthly cycle of Psalter-Chants will not prove to have been fruitlessly spent. Notwithstanding
unavoidable imperfections, and short-comings from an ideal standard of which they are fully
conscious, yet with the earnest hope that what is here offered may in some degree help forward
the highest and noblest of all aims in public Worship, the Editors submit their Work to the
consideration and, if it may be, acceptance of their brother Churchmen.

September, 1888.

POSTSCRIPT.

The lamented death the year before last of Sir Frederick Ouseley, when the present Work
was well-nigh finished, has left the task of its completion and final revision to his co-Editor and
former associate in similar labours. The views and designs herein of the deceased Editor, fully
understood and shared by his survivor, have been carried out, in the following pages, with all due
exactness and fidelity.

E. G. M.

September, 1891.

EXPLANATIONS AND SUGGESTIONS.

The present Work consists of two separate portions:

    I. The Voice Part : being the *Melody* of each Chant, for *Choir and Congregation.*

    II. The Organ Harmonies ; for *Instrumental* use only.

The former will be sung by the high and low voices—generally in combination, *i.e.*, in Octaves ; but also in alternation if desired, instead of the usual Dec. and Can. (*see* Psalm xxiv.).

The *Pitch* has been carefully chosen throughout, with due regard to average convenience ; yet the experienced Choirmaster, in concert with his Accompanist, may, in most cases, somewhat raise or lower it for Festal, Penitential, or other occasions. (*See examples among the Chants for Proper Psalms.*) In order to secure good Chanting it is necessary, 1st, to pronounce every syllable distinctly and deliberately, taking special care to sound all consonants ; 2ndly, to observe without exaggeration all necessary stops ; 3rdly, to avoid dropping the voice before stops and pauses ; and, 4thly, especially to avoid making a pause between the reciting-note and the rhythmical portion of the Chant. As to the pace at which the words are uttered, there should be as little difference as may be between the free and the measured portions of the Chant ; the *recitation* being somewhat more deliberate, the *inflection* somewhat quicker than is common. At the same time, the former should not degenerate into a tedious drawl, nor the latter be secularized by unseemly haste.

The *Pace* may well be governed by one simple rule ;—let it never be *faster* than will admit of the clear pronunciation of every word, together with as strict an observance of the Stops as is universal in good Reading, since Singing—a more artificial utterance—demands fuller scope for its proper performance ; otherwise it degenerates into mere gabble and unseemly patter. Further, *many* voices cannot possibly unite and move together so rapidly as can a few. Nor is *distance* between the component parts of a Choir and Congregation a consideration to be neglected, wherever a tendency exists towards excessive speed. Such a tendency seems to be prevalent at the present time, and is greatly to be deplored as being a serious hindrance to order and decorum, while evidencing wide divergence from the spirit (if not the letter) of our Prayer Book, from the teaching of holy Bishops and Pastors, and from that "*grave liveliness*" which may well distinguish, and set apart from all else, our acts and utterances in public worship. An occasional slight slackening or acceleration of the pace is, undoubtedly, a powerful means of drawing attention to special passages in the text, and of eliciting appropriate expression ; but this requires careful previous preparation, in order to create unity of thought and purpose among all concerned. Doubtless, one unvarying pace for *all* Psalms alike can hardly approve itself to the intelligence or devotional instincts of thoughtful worshippers, who will feel that such Psalms as the 22nd and 51st cannot with propriety be sung at the same cheerful speed as the 29th, 136th, and other similarly jubilant Psalms.

As to degrees of *Force*, the three simplest and most essential—Soft (*P.*), Medium (*M.*), Loud (*F.*), well defined in each singer's mind, and by habit become available at pleasure—will suffice to impart to chanting much of the Congregational relief and variety so vital to its due performance.

In all instances where *Change of Melody* in the course of a Psalm is proposed, an alternative plan is provided, that such change may be avoided when likely to prove embarrassing. It is believed, however, that the changes here indicated can always be readily mastered by a little preliminary practice, while their adoption will certainly tend to freshen interest and stimulate feeling, as well as to relieve any strain upon the vocal organs in the longer Psalms.

The *Organ Part* presents each Chant, usually in its original or accepted form, followed by one or more *changed* Harmonies. The latter (within the narrow limits available) are mainly designed to illustrate the Text, rather than merely to give musical colour and contrast to the Instrumental element,' desirable as *that* will always be. They are not obtruded on the notice of trained and ripe musicians, duly qualified to furnish their own diverse Harmonies. All arrangements of the Chants have been brought within the compass of a pair of hands, so as to be suitable for a small organ, or for a harmonium, as well as for moderately skilled players. The effect of these will be much enhanced by the employment, where possible, of differing *qualities* of Tone, as well as gradations of *power*, in constant observance of the varying character and sentiment of each Psalm or portion of a Psalm. Such attention to "light and shade" by the accompanist will quickly be caught and imitated by the singers, and, in conjunction with the significant use of changed Harmonies, cannot fail to further the object aimed at in the following pages. A dull and lifeless accompanist will as certainly act depressingly upon his singers as will one of an opposite spirit generate in them life, vigour, and heartiness. The chief burden is thus thrown, not improperly, upon his shoulders who is often the choirmaster, if not also the best musician of the parish. His duty is to guide and animate his forces, initiate with decision all changes of Chant, and supply, so far as may be, a truthful and suggestive enforcement of the Sacred Text. Assuredly there is no part of the daily Service of our Church in which the presence of a thoughtful and religious intelligence at the key-board is more urgently needful, or more highly to be prized, than in the chanting of the Psalter; nor (in connection with Congregational Singing) is there any choicer opportunity for instrumental alliance with voices, which (if but rarely picturesque) shall always be instructive, devotional, and elevating.

The friendly and valuable counsel long given to the Editors in the prosecution of their work, as well as various contributions thereto, from its inception to the last year of his life, by Sir G. A. Macfarren, must here be gratefully acknowledged. More recently (since the further heavy loss of its chief Editor) thanks are largely due to the Rev. Christopher Thompson, Vicar of Pensax, for untiring aid and advice, such as one in Holy Orders, and an expert on the subject of chanting, could most fittingly afford; and also to Dr. Mark J. Monk, of Truro Cathedral, both for practical suggestions and much timely help during its preparation and passage through the press.

Besides past obligations to numerous Contributors to the Editors' "Pointed Psalter" (the Chants from which are for the most part embodied in the present collection), hearty thanks are offered to the following Composers, who, with ready kindness, have severally permitted the insertion of not a few fresh Chants:—Sir G. J. Elvey; J. Barnby, F. Bentley, G. F. Cobb, J. Heywood, A. H. Littleton, H. Löhr, Walter Macfarren, C. J. B. Meacham, E. Prout, K. J. Pye, and S. Reay, Esqrs.; Dr. Bunnett, Dr. C. J. Frost, Dr. C. S. Heap, Dr. J. Naylor, and Dr. C. W. Pearce. Nor must the Chants by the late Rev. W. H. Havergal be passed by, without record of his own free permission for their use. Permission has also been liberally given for the use of a few copyright Chants, by A. H. Brown, Esq., from his "Anglican Psalter and Canticles"; H. Löhr, Esq., from his "London Chant Book"; and by W. A. Jefferson, Esq., from his "National Book of Hymn Tunes and Kyries." All Chants here acknowledged, as well as those now first printed, are marked thus (†) in the Index.

Michaelmas, 1891.

INDEX.

	Original Key.	Transposed Key.	No.
Frost, E. ...	Bb	A	82
†Frost, Dr. C. J. ...	Bb		186
Fussell	G	F	294
Garland, W. H. ...	E	D	246
Garrett, Dr. G. ...	C	Bb	68
" " ...	D	C	179
Gibbons, Dr. C. ...	G	F	135
Gilbert, Dr. W. B. ..	F		57
" " ...	Ab	F	67
Goldwin, J. ...	G minor	F# minor	102
Goodson, R. ...	D	C	20
Goss, Sir J. ...	E minor	D minor	10
" " ...	A minor	G minor	45
† " ...	G		239
Greene, Dr. M. ...	A	G	279
†Hackett ..	Bb	A	278
†Havergal, Rev. H. E....	D		171
Havergal, Rev. W. H.	A	G	28
" "	D	C	36
† " "	Bb	A	42
† " "	F	D	84
† " "	A minor	F minor	88
† " "	C		89
† " "	E minor	D minor	113
" "	E	D	130
" "	Bb		136
" "	F		184
† " "	Eb	D	226
" "	D		252
" "	C	Bb	298
" "	D	C	306
Hayes, Dr. W. ...	C	Bb	56
" " ...	D		103
" " ...	A	G	168
" " ...	D	C	219
Hayes, Dr. P. ...	E	Eb	72
" " ...	F	Eb	232
†Heap, Dr. C. S. ...	Ab	G	164
Heathcote, Rev. G. ...	Bb	A	127
Helmore, Rev. T. ...	F	E	229
Hervey, Rev. F. A. J....	Eb		29
†Heywood, J. ...	G minor		153
†Hiles, Dr. H. ...	E	D	162
" ...	Ab	G	182
Hindle, J. ...	G	F	53
" ...	A	Ab	254
Hine, W. ...	G minor		17
" ...	G	F	141
Hopkins, Dr. E. J. ...	Eb	D	12
" " ...	Bb	Ab	260
Humphrey, P. ...	C	Bb	9
Jones, J. ...	C	Bb	58
Kelway, T. ...	D	C	14
" ...	G minor	F# minor	77
Kempton, T. ...	Bb	A	201
King, C. ...	G	Eb	259
" ...	B minor	G minor	284
Lamb, B.... ...	F	Eb and E	196
Langdon, R. ...	G minor	E minor	119
Lee, W. ...	G	F	90
" ...	D		166
†Littleton, A. H. ...	F	Eb	285
†Löhr, Harvey ...	D	Bb	295
Macfarren, Sir G. A....	D	C	22
" " ...	A	G	47
" " ...	C	Bb	55

	Original Key.	Transposed Key.	No.
Macfarren, Sir G. A....	D		98
" " ...	Bb	G	120
" " ...	Bb	G	163
" " ...	A minor	G minor	170
† " " ...	E minor		204
" " ...	Eb	D	216
" " ...	G	F	220
" " ...	Ab	G	223
" " ...	Bb	Ab	233
† " " ...	G	F	242
† " " ...	A	Ab	257
† " " ...	F minor		264
" " ...	C minor	B minor	283
†Macfarren, Walter ...	G		205
Matthews, Rev. T. R.	G		26
†Meacham, C. J. B. ...	Ab	A	99
† " " ...	D	C	177
Monk, Henry T. ...	F	Eb	230
†Monk, E. G. ...	E		3
† " ...	A		4
" ...	A minor	G minor	7
† " ...	Eb		18
† " ...	D		38
" ...	Db	D	40
" ...	A		44
† " ...	D		46
† " ...	Ab		50
" ...	D minor	C minor	54
" ...	G		60
† " ...	F minor [Ab major]		70
† " ...	A	Ab	73
" ...	G		83
" ...	G	F	96
† " ...	C		104
" ...	D	C	115
† " ...	A		129
" ...	E minor [G major]		146
† " ...	E		149
" ...	G		156
" ...	D	C	161
" ...	A minor	G minor	167
† " ...	D		173
" ...	Ab	G	174
† " ...	G		191
" ...	Ab	G	218
" ...	Eb	D	224
" ...	Bb		243
† " ...	G minor	F# minor	251
" ...	D minor	C minor	265
" ...	D		268
" ...	E	D	280
" ...	A	F	296
" ...	A		305
† " ...	Eb	D	317
†Monk, Dr. Mark J. ...	G		39
† " " ...	A		277
† " ...	C		304
Nares, Dr. J. ...	A	G	63
" (From) ...	D	C	198
†Naylor, Dr. J. ...	G minor		11
" ...	D	C	118
†Novello, Vincent ...	A	G	193
†Ouseley, Rev. Sir F.A.G.		C	15
" "	G	F	16
" "	Bb	Ab	30
" "	D	C	91

Day 1.—Morning.

1 (a). Venite. *v. 1 to 7: and* Gloria Patri.

Sir G. J. Elvey.

1 (b). *v. 8 to 11:*

2 (a). Psalm i. *v. 1 to 4: and 7 to end.*

T. Tallis.

2 (b). *v. 5, 6:*

3 (a). Ps. ii. *v. 1 to 3: and G. P.*

E. G. Monk.

3 (b). *v. 4 to 6:*

3 (c). *v. 7 to 9:*

3 (d). *v. 10 to 12:*

4 (a). Ps. iii. *v. 1, 2:*

E. G. M.

4 (b). *v. 3 to end.*

5 (a). Ps. iv. *v. 1 to 6: and 9 to end.*

R. Farrant.

5 (b). *v. 7, 8:*

6 (a). Ps. v. *v. 1, 2 : 7, 8 : and 12 to end.*

Dr. S. Elvey.

6 (b). *v. 3 to 6; 9 to 11:*

(1)

Day 1.—Evening.

————FIRST SET.————

7 (a).   Ps. vi. *v.* 1 *to* 7: *and* G. P.

7 (b).   *v.* 8 *to* 10:

E. G. Monk.

8 (a).   Ps. vii. *v.* 1 *to* 5: *and* 18 *to end.*

From Dr. Aldrich.

8 (b).   *v.* 6 *to* 10:

8 (c).   *v.* 11 *to* 17:

9 (a).   Ps. viii. *v.* 1 *to* 3: *and* 9 *to end.*

9 (b).   *v.* 4 *to* 8:

P. Humphreys.

————SECOND SET.————

10 (a).   Ps. vi. *v.* 1 *to* 7: *and* G. P.

10 (b).   *v.* 8 *to* 10:

Sir. J. Goss.

11 (a).   Ps. vii. *v.* 1 *to* 5: 11 *to* 17: *and* G. P.

11 (b).   *v.* 6 *to* 10: 18:

Dr. Naylor.

12 (a).   Ps. viii. *v.* 1 *to* 3: *and* 9 *to end.*

12 (b).   *v.* 4 *to* 8:

Dr. E. J. Hopkins.

(2)

Day 2.—Morning.

13 (a). Venite, v. 1 to 7: and G. P.

Dr. T. A. WALMISLEY.

13 (b). v. 8 to 11:

14 (a). Ps. ix. v. 1 to 12: and 19 to end.

T. KELWAY.

14 (b). v. 13 to 18:

15 (a). Ps. x. v. 1 to 12: and 18 to end.

Rev. Sir F. OUSELEY.

15 (b). v. 13 to 17:

16 (a.) Ps. xi. v. 1 to 3: and 8 to end.

F. A. G. O.

16 (b). v. 4 to 7:

Day 2.—Evening.

17 (a). Ps. xii. v. 1 to 4: and 7 to end.

W. HINE.

17 (b). v. 5, 6:

18 (a). Ps. xiii. v. 1, 2: and 5 to end.

E. G. MONK.

18 (b). v. 3, 4:

19 (a). Ps. xiv. v. 1 to 8: and G. P.

J. CORFE.

19 (b). v. 9 to 11:

(3)

Day 3.—Morning.

20 (a).   Venite, v. 1 to 7 : and G. P.

From R. GOODSON.

20 (b).   v. 8 to 11 :

21 (a).   Ps. xv. v. 1, 2 : and 7 to end.

Rev. Dr. DYKES.

21 (b).   v. 3 to 6 :

22 (a).   Ps. xvi. v. 1 to 12 :

Sir G. A. MACFARREN.

22 (b).   G. P.

Or 23 (a).   Ps. xvi. 1 to 7 : and G. P.

S. REAY.

23 (b).   v. 8 to 12 :

24 (a).   Ps. xvii. v. 1 to 5 : and 13 to end.

Right Rev. Bishop TURTON.

24 (b).   v. 6 to 12 :

(4)

Day 3.—Morning.

25 (a). [Or 20.]   Venite, *v.* 1 *to* 7 : *and* G. P.

From W. BYRDE.

25 (b).   *v.* 8 *to* 11 :

26 (a).   Ps. xv. *v.* 1, 2 : *and* 7 *to* end.

REV. T. R. MATTHEWS.

26 (b).   *v.* 3 *to* 6 :

27 (a).   Ps. xvi. *v.* 1 *to* 7 : *and* G. P.

Adapted.

27 (b).   *v.* 8 *to* 12 :

28 (a).   Ps. xvii. *v.* 1 *to* 5 : *and* 13 *to* end.

REV. W. H. HAVERGAL.

28 (b).   *v.* 6 *to* 12 :

Day 3.—Evening.

FIRST SET.

29. Ps. xviii. *v. 1 to 6 : and 47 to end.*

Rev. F. A. J. HERVEY.

30. *v. 7 to 15 : 31 to 46 :*

Rev. Sir F. OUSELEY.

31. *v. 16 to 30 :*

Dr. W. CROTCH.

SECOND SET.

30 (a). Ps. xviii. *v. 1 to 6 : 31 to 46 : and G. P.*

Transposed.

F. A. G. O.

30 (b). *v. 7 to 15 :*

30 (c). *v. 16 to 30 :*

30 (d). *v. 47 to 51 :*

(6)

Day 4.—Morning.

──────── FIRST SET. ────────

32 (a).   Venite, *v.* 1 *to* 7 : *and* G. P.

32 (b).   *v.* 8 *to* 11 :

Rev. W. Tucker.

33 (a).   Ps. xix. *v.* 1 *to* 11 : *and* 15 *to end.*

33 (b).   *v.* 12 *to* 14 :

J. Battishill.

34 (a).   Ps. xx. *v.* 1 *to* 5 : 7, 8 : *and* G. P.

34 (b).   *v.* 6 : 9 :

J. Travers.

35 (a).   Ps. xxi. *v.* 1 *to* 7 : *and* 13 *to end.*

35 (b).   *v.* 8 *to* 12 :

Dr. T. S. Dupuis.

Or **36 (a).** Ps. xxi. *v.* 1 *to* 7 : *and* 13 *to end.*

36 (b).   *v.* 8 *to* 12 :

Rev. W. H. Havergal.

(7)

─────── SECOND SET. ───────

37 (a).   Venite, *v.* 1 *to* 7: *and* G. P.

D. PURCELL.

37 (b).   *v.* 8 *to* 11.

38 (a).   Ps. xix. *v.* 1 *to* 11: *and* 15 *to end.*   **38 (b).**   *v.* 12 *to* 14:

E. G. MONK.

39 (a).   Ps. xx. *v.* 1 *to* 5: 7, 8: *and* G. P.   **39 (b).**   *v.* 6: 9:

DR. MARK J. MONK.

40 (a).   Ps. xxi. *v.* 1 *to* 7: *and* 13 *to end.*   **40 (b).**   *v.* 8 *to* 12:

E. G. M.

(8)

Day 4.—Evening.

——FIRST SET.——

41 (a).   Ps. xxii. *v. 1 to 21 : and* G. P.

Dr. J. Blow.

42.   *v. 22 to end.*   Or **41 (b).**   *v. 22 to 32 :*

Rev. W. H. Havergal.

43, *Follows* **42.**   Ps. xxiii.   **44,** *Follows* **41 (b).**   Ps. xxiii.

J. Barrow.   E. G. Monk.

——SECOND SET.——

45.   Ps. xxii. *v. 1 to 21 :*

Sir J. Goss.

46.   *v. 22 to end.*

E. G. M.

47.   Ps. xxiii.

Sir G. A. Macfarren.

(9)

Day 5.—Morning.

48 (a). Venite, *v. 1 to 7: and G. P.*

48 (b). *v. 8 to 11:*

W. V. WALLACE.

49 (a). Ps. XXIV. *v. 1 to 6:*

Dr. S. ARNOLD.

49 (b). *v. 7: 9: and G. P.*

49 (c). *v. 8: 10:*

(TREBLES ONLY.) FULL.

* If sung by Men only, or Full, play Bass (*——*) 8ve lower.

50 (a). Ps. XXV. *v. 1 to 4: 7 to 14: and 19 to end.*

50 (b). *v. 5, 6: 15 to 18:*

E. G. MONK.

Or **51 (a).** Ps. XXV. *v. 1 to 4: 7 to 14: and 19 to end.*

51 (b). *v. 5, 6: 15 to 18:*

A. R. REINAGLE.

52 (a). Ps. XXVI. *v. 1 to 5: 9 to 11: and G. P.*

52 (b). *v. 6 to 8: 12:*

W. DYCE.

(10)

Day 5.—Evening.

53 (a). Ps. xxvii. *v.* 1 *to* 7 : *and* 15 *to end.*

J. HINDLE.

53 (b). *v.* 8 *to* 14 :

54 (a). Ps. xxviii. 1 *to* 6 :

E. G. MONK.

54 (b). *v.* 7 *to end.*

Major.

55 (a). Ps. xxix. *v.* 1 *to* 8 : *and* G. P.

Sir G. A. MACFARREN.

55 (b). *v.* 9, 10 :

Day 6.—Morning.

56 (a). Venite, *v.* 1 *to* 7 : *and* G. P.

Dr. W. HAYES.

56 (b). *v.* 8 *to* 11 :

57 (a). Ps. xxx. *v.* 1 *to* 6 : *and* 12 *to end.*

Dr. W. B. GILBERT.

57 (b). *v.* 7 *to* 11 :

58 (a). Ps. xxxi. *v.* 1 *to* 9 : *and* 21 *to end.*

J. JONES.

59 *v.* 10 *to* 20 :

Dr. T. S. DUPUIS.

Or 58 (b). *v.* 10 *to* 20.

Day 6.—Evening.

60 (a). Ps. xxxii. v. 1, 2 : and 7 to end.

60 (b). v. 3 to 6 :

E. G. Monk.

Or 61 (a). Ps. xxxii. v. 1, 2 : and 7 to end.

61 (b). v. 3 to 6 :

Dr. Bunnett.

62 (a). Ps. xxxiii. v. 1 to 9 : and 19 to end.

62 (b). v. 10 to 18 :

Sir G. J. Elvey.

63 (a). Ps. xxxiv. v. 1 to 7 : and 15 to end.

63 (b). v. 8 to 14 :

Dr. J. Nares.

Day 7.—Morning.

-----FIRST SET.-----

64 (a). Venite, v. 1 to 7 : and G. P.

64 (b). v. 8 to 11 :

T. Tallis.

65. Ps. xxxv. v. 1 to 10 : and 19 to end.

66. v. 11 to 18 :

Dr. E. F. Rimbault.

Anonymous.

67. Ps. xxxvi. v. 1 to 4 : 10 to 12 :

68. v. 5 to 9 : and G. P.

Dr. W. B. Gilbert.

Dr. G. Garrett.

Day 7.—Morning.

SECOND SET.

69 (a). Venite, v. 1 to 7 : and G. P.

69 (b). v. 8 to 11 :

E. J. BELLERBY.

70 (a). Ps. XXXV. v. 1 to 8 : 11 to 16 : 19 to 26 :

70 (b). v. 9, 10 : 17, 18 : and 27 to end.

E. G. MONK.

71 (a). Ps. XXXVI. v. 1 to 4 : and 11 to end.

71 (b). v. 5 to 10 :

G. H. E. MASSY DAWSON.

Day 7.—Evening.

FIRST SET.

72 (a). Ps. XXXVII. v. 1 to 11 : 33 to 36 : and 40 to end.

72 (b). v. 12 to 20 : 37 to 39 :

DR. P. HAYES.

72 (c). v. 21, 22 :

73. v. 23 to 32 :

E. G. M.

SECOND SET.

74 (a). Ps. XXXVII. v. 1 to 11 : 23 to 32 : and 40 to end.

FROM BRAILESFORD.

74 (b). v. 12 to 20 : 33 to 36 :

74 (c). v. 21, 22 : 37 to 39 :

Day 8.—Morning.

75 (a).   Venite v. 1 to 7 : and G. P.

W. BOWER.

75 (b).   v. 8 to 11:

76 (a).   Ps. xxxviii. v. 1 to 10 : and 15 to end.

R. FARRANT.

76 (b).   v. 11 to 14.

Or 77 (a).   Ps. xxxviii. v. 1 to 10 : and 15 to end.

T. KELWAY.

77 (b).   v. 11 to 14.

78 (a).   Ps. xxxix. v. 1 to 4 : 8 to 12 : and G. P.

REV. W. FELTON.

78 (b).   v. 5 to 7 : 13 to 15:

79 (a).   Ps. xl. v. 1 to 13 : and 19 to end.

E. FROST.

79 (b).   v. 14 to 18:

Day 8.—Evening.

———FIRST SET.———

80 (a). Ps. xli. *v.* 1 *to* 3 : *and* 10 *to end.*

80 (b). *v.* 4 *to* 9 :

Dr. T. S. Dupuis.

81 (a). Ps. xlii. *v.* 1 *to* 5 : 8 *to* 13 : *and* G. P.

81 (b). *v.* 6, 7 : 14, 15 :

Dr. C. W. Corfe.

82 (a). Ps. xliii. *v.* 1 *to* 4 : *and* G. P.

82 (b). *v.* 5, 6 :

E. Frost.

———SECOND SET.———

83 (a). Ps. xli. *v.* 1 *to* 3 : *and* 10 *to end.*

83 (b). *v.* 4 *to* 9 :

E. G. Monk.

84 (a). Ps. xlii. *v.* 1 *to* 5 : 8 *to* 13 : *and* G. P.

84 (b). *v.* 6, 7 : 14, 15 :

Rev. W. H. Havergal.

85. Ps. xliii.

Sir J. Stainer.

(15)

Day 9.—Morning.

86 (*a*).   Venite, *v. 1 to 7 : and G. P.*

FROM W. BYRDE.

86 (*b*).   *v. 8 to 11 :*

87 (*a*).   Ps. xliv. *v. 1 to 9 : 23 : and 26 to end.*

H. WICKS.

88 (*a*).   *v. 10 to 17 :*

REV. W. H. HAVERGAL.

88 (*b*).   *v. 18 to 22 :*

87 (*b*).   *v. 24, 25 :*

Also (*ad lib.*), 87 (*a*) and (*b*) throughout Ps. xliv. ; as directed for 89 (*a*) and (*b*).

Or 89 (*a*). Ps. xliv. *v. 1 to 9 : 18 to 20 : 23 : and 26 to end.*

REV. W. H. HAVERGAL.

89 (*b*).   *v. 10 to 17 : 21, 22 : 24, 25 :*

90 (*a*).   Ps. xlv. *v. 1 to 10 : and 17 to end.*

W. LEE.

90 (*b*).   *v. 11 to 16 :*

91 (*a*).   Ps. xlvi. *v. 1 to 6 : 8 to 10 : and G. P.*

REV. SIR F. OUSELEY.

91 (*b*).   *v. 7 : 11 :*

Day 9.—Evening.

————FIRST SET.————

92 (a). Ps. xlvii. *v.* 1 *to* 4 : *and* 8 *to end.*

92 (b). *v.* 5 *to* 7 :

Dr. E. Ayrton.

93 (a). Ps. xlviii. *v.* 1, 2 : *and* 8 *to end.*

93 (b). *v.* 3 *to* 7 :

Dr. E. F. Rimbault.

94 (a). Ps. xlix. *v.* 1 *to* 4 : *and* 12 *to end.*

94 (b). *v.* 5 *to* 11 :

Anon.

————SECOND SET.————

95 (a). Ps. xlvii. *v.* 1 *to* 4 : *and* 8 *to end.*

95 (b). *v.* 5 *to* 7 :

S. Reay.

96 (a). Ps. xlviii. *v.* 1, 2 : *and* 8 *to end.*

96 (b). *v.* 3 *to* 7 :

E. G. Monk

97 (a). Ps. xlix. *v.* 1 *to* 4 : *and* 12 *to end.*

97 (b). *v.* 5 *to* 11 :

Dr. T. A. Walmisley.

Day 10.—Morning.

98 (a). Venite, v. 1 to 7 : and G. P.

Sir G. A. MACFARREN.

98 (b). v. 8 to 11 :

99 (a). Ps. l. v. 1 to 6 : and 22 to end

C. J. B. MEACHAM.

99 (b). v. 7 to 15 :

100. v. 16 to 21 :

Or 99 (c). v. 16 to 21 :

Or 101 (a). Ps. l. v. 1 to 6 : and 22 to end.

Dr. W. TURNER.

101 (b). v. 7 to 15 :

101 (c). v. 16 to 21 :

102 (a). Ps. ll. v. 1 to 13 : and 18 to end.

From J. GOLDWIN.

102 (b). v. 14 to 17 :

103 (a). Ps. lll. v. 1, 2 : and 7 to end.

Dr. W. HAYES.

103 (b). v. 3 to 6 :

(18)

Day 10.—Evening.

104 (a).   Ps. liii. v. 1 to 5 ; and G. P.

104 (b).   v. 6 to 8 :

E. G. Monk.

105 (a).   Ps. liv. v. 1 to 3 ; and 6 to end.

105 (b).   v. 4, 5.

J. T. Cooper.

106 (a).   Ps. lv. v. 1 to 8 :

J. Weldon.

106 (b).   v. 9 to 13 :

106 (c).   v. 14 to 16 :

107.   v. 17 to end.

T. E. Aylward.

Or 106 (d).   v. 17 to end.

(19)

108 (a). Venite, v. 1 to 7: and G. P.

108 (b). v. 8 to 11:

Ancient.

109 (a). Ps. lvi. v. 1, 2: 5 to 8: and 12 to end.

109 (b). v. 3, 4: 9 to 11:

J. Barnby.

110 (b). Ps. lvii. v. 1 to 5:

110 (a). v. 6 to end.

E. J. Bellerby.

111 (a). Ps. lviii. v. 1, 2: 6 to 8: and G. P.

111 (b). v. 3 to 5: 9, 10:

Dr. E. F. Rimbault.

112 (a). Ps. lix. 1 to 5: 8 to 13: and 16 to end.

112 (b). v. 6, 7: 14, 15:

F. Bentley.

113 (a). Ps. lx. v. 1 to 5: and 9 to end.

113 (b). v. 6 to 8:

Rev. W. H. Havergal.

114 (a). Ps. lxi. v. 1 to 4: and G. P.

114 (b). v. 5 to 8:

Dr. C. W. Corfe.

Day 12.—Morning.

115 (a). Venite, *v. 1 to 7 : and* G. P.

115 (b). *v. 8 to 11:*

E. G. MONK.

116 (a). Ps. lxii. *v. 1 to 8: and* G. P.

116 (b). *v. 9 to 12:*

Anon.

Or 117 (a). Ps. lxii. *v. 1 to 8: and* G. P.

117 (b). *v. 9 to 12:*

Right Rev. Bishop TURTON.

118 (a). Ps. lxiii. *v. 1 to 3: and 10 to end.*

118 (b). *v. 4 to 9:*

Dr. J. NAYLOR.

119. Ps. lxiv.

R. LANGDON.

Or 120. Ps. lxiv.

Sir G. A. MACFARREN

(21)

C

Day 12.—Evening.

121 (a). Ps. lxv. v. 1 to 4 : and 9 to end.

Dr. C. W. Pearce.

121 (b). v. 5 to 8 :

122 (a). Ps. lxvi. v. 1 to 8 : and 14 to end.

Dr. T. A. Walmisley.

122 (b). v. 9 to 13 :

123 (a). Ps. lxvii. v. 1, 2 : 4 : 6, 7 :

Dr. C. Steggall.

123 (b). v. 3 ; 5 : and G. P.

Day 13.—Morning.

——FIRST SET.——

124 (a). Venite, v. 1 to 7 : and G. P.

Ancient.

124 (b). v. 8 to 11 :

125. Ps. lxviii. v. 1 to 6 : 19 to 23 :

From W. Russell.

126 (a). v. 7 to 14 ; 24 to 31 ; and G. P.

Dr. E. F. Rimbault.

126 (b). v. 15 to 18 : 32 to 35 :

(22)

Day 13.—Morning.

SECOND SET.

127 (a). Venite, *v.* 1 *to* 7 : *and* G. P.

127 (b). *v.* 8 *to* 11 :

Rev. G. Heathcote.

126 (a). Ps. lxviii. *v.* 1 *to* 18 : 24 *to* 31 : *and* G. P.

126 (c). *v.* 19 *to* 23 :

Dr. E. F. Rimbault.

126 (b). *v.* 32 *to* 35 :

Day 13.—Evening.

FIRST SET.

128 (a). Ps. lxix. *v.* 1 *to* 12 : 20 *to* 29 :

128 (b). *v.* 13 *to* 19 :

T. Tallis.

129. *v.* 30 *to end.*

Or 128 (c). *v.* 30 *to end.*

E. G. Monk.

130. Ps. lxx.

Rev. W. H. Havergal.

Day 13.—Evening.

131 (a).   Ps. lxix. *v. 1 to 12 : 20 to 29 :*

131 (b).   *v. 13 to 19 :*

Rev. Sir F. Ouseley.

132.   *v. 30 to end.*

Major.

Or **131 (c).**   *v. 30 to end.*

133.   Ps. lxx.

G. F. Cobb.

Day 14.—Morning.

134 (a).   Venite, *v. 1 to 7 ; and* G. P.

134 (b).   *v. 8 to 11 :*

Dr. W. Crotch.

135 (a).   Ps. lxxi. *v. 1 to 5 ; and 12 to end,*

135 (b).   *v. 6 to 11 :*

Dr. C. Gibbons.

136 (a).   Ps. lxxii. *v. 1 to 11 ; and* G. P.

136 (b).   *v. 12 to 17 :*

Rev. W. H. Havergal.

136 (c).   *v. 18, 19 :*

Day 14.—Evening.

137 (a).   Ps. lxxiii. *v.* 1 *to* 14 : *and* 22 *to end.*

J. FOSTER.

138.   *v.* 15 *to* 21 :

Dr. PRING.

Or **137** (b).   *v.* 15 *to* 21 :

139.   Ps. lxxiv. *v.* 1 *to* 12 : *and* 19 *to end.*

Sir W. S. BENNETT.

140.   *v.* 13 *to* 18 :

Rev. Sir F. OUSELEY.

Or **141** (a).   Ps. lxxiv. *v.* 1 *to* 12 : *and* 19 *to end.*

W. HINE.

141 (b).   *v.* 13 *to* 18 :

Or, for v. 13 *to* 18, *use* **140** *instead of* **141** (b).

(25)

Day 15.—Morning.

37 (a).   Venite, v. 1 to 7 : and G. P.   37 (b).   v. 8 to 11 :

D. PURCELL.

142 (a).   Ps. lxxv. v. 1 to 4 : and 11 to end.   142 (b).   v. 5 to 10 :

Dr. E. F. RIMBAULT.

143 (a).   Ps. lxxvi. v. 1 to 6 ; and 10 to end.   143 (b).   v. 7 to 9 :

J. BATTISHILL

144.   Ps. lxxvii. v. 1 to 9 :

Dr. T. S. DUPUIS.

145.   v. 10 to end.

Dr. W. CROTCH.

Or 146 (b).   Ps. lxxvii. v. 1 to 9 :   146 (a).   v. 10 to end.

E. G. MONK.

Day 15.—Evening.

————FIRST SET.————

147 (a). Ps. lxxviii. *v.* 1 *to* 12 :

Anon.

147 (b). *v.* 13 *to* 17 :

148. *v.* 18 *to* 21 : 32 *to* 44 :

Rev. Sir F. Ouseley.

149. *v.* 22 *to* 31 : 45 *to* 52 :

E. G. Monk.

150(a). *v.* 53 *to* 56 : and 66 *to end.*

From W. Walond.

151 (a). *v.* 57 *to* 65 :

From Wanless.

150(b). G. P. (*ad lib.*)

————SECOND SET.————

150(a). Ps. lxxviii. *v.* 1 *to* 12 : 53 *to* 56 : and 66 *to end.*

From W. Walond.

150(c). *v.* 13 *to* 17 : 22 *to* 31 :

150(d). *v.* 18 *to* 21 : 57 *to* 65 :

151 (a). *v.* 32 *to* 44 :

151 (b). *v.* 45 *to* 52 :

From Wanless.

Or, as follows, without change of Melody ;

| *v.* 1 *to* 12 : 53 *to* 56 : *v.* 66 *to end.* } 150 (a). | *v.* 13 *to* 17 : 22 *to* 31 : *v.* 45 *to* 52 : 57 *to* 65 : } 150 (c). | *v.* 18 *to* 21 : *v.* 32 *to* 44 : } 150 (d). |

(27)

Day 16.—Morning.

152 (a).   Venite, *v.* 1 *to* 7 : *and* G. P.

152 (b).   *v.* 8 *to* 11.

Sir R. P. STEWART.

153 (a).   Ps. lxxix. *v.* 1 *to* 7 : *and* 14 *to end.*

153 (b).   *v.* 8 *to* 13 :

J. HEYWOOD.

154 (a).   Ps. lxxx. *v.* 1 *to* 11 : *and* 17 *to end.*

154 (b).   *v.* 12 *to* 16 :

Dr. E. F. RIMBAULT.

155 (a).   lxxxi. *v.* 1 *to* 11 : *and* G. P.

155 (b).   *v.* 12 *to* 17 :

Sir R. P. STEWART.

Or **156 (a).** Ps. lxxxi. *v.* 1 *to* 11 : *and* G. P.

156 (b).   *v.* 12 *to* 17 :

E. G. MONK.

157 (a). Ps. lxxxii. *v. 1 to 4: and 8 to end.*

157 (b). *v. 5 to 7:*

R. S. BURTON.

158 (a). Ps. lxxxiii. *v. 1 to 8: and 13 to end.*

158 (b). *v. 9 to 12:*

J. TRAVERS.

159 (a). Ps. lxxxiv. *v. 1 to 4: and 9 to end.*

159 (b). *v. 5 to 8:*

From W. RUSSELL.

160 (a). Ps. lxxxv. *v. 1 to 3: and 8 to end.*

160 (b). *v. 4 to 7:*

Dr. W. CROTCH.

Or **161 (a).** Ps. lxxxv. *v. 1 to 3: and 8 to end.*

161 (b). *v. 4 to 7:*

E. G. MONK.

(29)

Day 17.—Morning.

162 (a). Venite, v. 1 to 7; and G. P.

162 (b). v. 8 to 11.

Dr. H. Hiles.

163. Ps. lxxxvi. v. 1 to 7; and 14 to end.

164. v. 8 to 13:

Sir G. A. Macfarren.

Dr. C. S. Heap.

Or 165 (a). Ps. lxxxvi. v. 1 to 13; and G. P.

165 (b). v. 14 to 17:

Sir G. J. Elvey.

166. Ps. lxxxvii.

From W. Lee.

167 (a). Ps. lxxxviii. v. 1 to 9; and 13 to end.

167 (b). v. 10 to 12:

E. G. Monk.

(30)

Day 17.—Evening.

———FIRST SET.———

168 (a). Ps. lxxxix. v. 1 to 4 : and 16 to 19 :

168 (b). v. 5 to 15 :

Dr. W. Hayes.

169 (a). v. 20 to 30 ; 33 to 36 :

169 (b). v. 31, 32 :

W. Dyce.

170(a). v. 37 to 44 : 49 :

170(b). v. 45 to 48 :

Sir G. A. Macfarren.

170 (c). v. 50 :

f Slower.

168 (a). G. P.

———SECOND SET.———

168 (a). Ps. lxxxix. v. 1 to 19 ; 33 to 36 : and G. P.

168 (b). v. 20 to 32 :

Dr. W. Hayes.

168 (c). v. 37 to 44 : 49 :

168 (d). v. 45 to 48 :

168 (e). v. 50 :

168 (f). G. P. (ad lib.)

(31)

Day 18.—Morning.

171 (a).   Venite, *v.* 1 *to* 7 : *and* G. P.

Rev. H. E. HAVERGAL.

171 (b).   *v.* 8 *to* 11 :

172 (a).   Ps. xc. *v.* 1 *to* 6 : *and* 13 *to end.*

Dr. W. CROFT.

172 (b).   *v.* 7 *to* 12 :

173 (a).   Ps. xci. *v.* 1 *to* 9 : *and* 14 *to end.*

E. G. M.

173 (b).   *v.* 10 *to* 13 :

174 (a).   Ps. xcii. *v.* 1 *to* 6 : *and* 9 *to end.*

E. G. MONK.

174 (b).   *v.* 7, 8 :

Day 18.—Evening.

———FIRST SET.———

175.   **Ps. xciii.**

Dr. W. DIXON.

176 (a).   **Ps. xciv.** *v.* 1, 2 : 8 *to* 11 :   **176 (b).**   *v.* 3 *to* 7 :

Rev. Sir F. OUSELEY.

Or, without change, **176** (*a*). *v.* 1, 2 : *and* **12** *to end.*   **176** (*b*). *v.* 3 *to* 11 :

177.   *v.* 12 *to end.*

C. J. B. MEACHAM.

———SECOND SET.———

178.   **Ps. xciii.**

Dr. T. A. WALMISLEY.

179 (a).   **Ps. xciv.** *v.* 1 *to* 11 : *and* G. P.   **179 (b).**   *v.* 12 *to* 23 :

Dr. G. GARRETT.

Day 19.—Morning.

180 (a). Ps. xcv v. 1 to 7 : and G. P.

180 (b). v. 8 to 11 :

Ancient.

181 (a). Ps. xcvi. v. 1 to 12 : and G. P.

181 (b). v. 13 :

Dr. J. Alcock.

182 (a). Ps. xcvii. v. 1 to 9 ; and 12 to end.

182 (b). v. 10, 11 :

Dr. H. Hiles.

Day 19.—Evening.

183 (a). Ps. xcviii. v. 1 to 4 : and 8 to end.

183 (b). v. 5 to 7 :

Dr. J. Pring.

184 (a). Ps. xcix. v. 1 to 4 : 6 to 8 : and G. P.

184 (b). v. 5 : 9 :

Rev. W. H. Havergal.

185. Ps. c.

Or 186. Ps. c.

J. Darnby.

Dr. C. J. Frost.

187. Ps. ci.

Or 188. Ps. ci.

Taylor.

Dr. E. F. Rimbault.

189 (a).   Venite, *v.* 1 *to* 7 : *and* G. P.

Anonymous.

189 (b).   *v.* 8 *to* 11 :

190.   Ps. cii. *v.* 1 *to* 11 : *and* 23 *to* end.

Or **190** *throughout* Ps. cii.

Dr. W. Crotch.

191.   *v.* 12 *to* 22 :

E. G. M.

Or **192.**   *v.* 23 *to* end.

Major.

Dr. W. Crotch.

Or **193 (a).** Ps. cii. *v.* 1 *to* 11 : *and* 23 *to* end.

V. Novello.

193 (b).   *v.* 12 *to* 22 :

194 (a).   Ps. ciii. *v.* 1 *to* 13 : *and* 17 *to* end.

J. Travers.

194 (b).   *v.* 14 *to* 16 :

(35)

Day 20.—Evening.

FIRST SET.

195 (a). Ps. civ. v. 1 to 4 : 24 to 30 ; and 33 to end.

195 (b). *v. 5 to 10 :*

Rev. Sir F. Ouseley

196 (a). *v. 11 to 18 : 23 :*

196 (b). *v. 19 to 22 :*

B. Lamb.

195 (c). *v. 31, 32 :*

SECOND SET.

196 (a). Ps. civ. v 1 to 4 : 24 to 30 ; and G. P.

196 (c). *v. 5 to 10 : 19 to 23 ; 31 to 35 :*

Tr.

B. Lamb.

196 (d). *v. 11 to 18 :*

(36)

Day 21.—Morning.

FIRST SET.

20 (a). Venite, *v.* 1 *to* 7: *and* G. P.

20 (b). *v.* 8 *to* 11:

From R. Goodson.

197. Ps. cv. *v.* 1 *to* 15: *and* 36 *to end.*

Rev. Sir F. Ouseley.

198 (a). *v.* 16 *to* 22: 26 *to* 35:

198 (b). *v.* 23 *to* 25:

Dr. J. Nares.

SECOND SET.

199 (a). Ps. cv. *v.* 1 *to* 15: *and* 36 *to end.*

200. *v.* 16 *to* 35:

Dr. W. Turner.

Sir G. J. Elvey.

THIRD SET.

199 (a). Ps. cv. *v.* 1 *to* 15: *and* 41 *to end.*

199 (b). *v.* 16 *to* 25:

Dr. W. Turner.

199 (c). *v.* 26, 27:

199 (d). *v.* 28 *to* 31:

199 (e). *v.* 32 *to* 35:

199 (f). *v.* 36 *to* 40:

(37)

D

Day 21.—Evening.

FIRST SET.

201 (a). Ps. cvi. *v.* 1 *to* 5 : *and* 46 *to end.*

T. Kempton.

202 (a). *v.* 6 *to* 12 : 28 *to* 33 : 39 *to* 42 : 45 :   **202 (b).** *v.* 13 *to* 27 :

Dr. W. Crotch.

202 (c). *v.* 34 *to* 38 :   **202 (d).** *v.* 43, 44 :

SECOND SET.

201 (a). Ps. cvi. *v.* 1 *to* 5 : 8 *to* 12 : *and* 43 *to end.*   **201 (b).** *v.* 6, 7 : 13 *to* 42 :

T. Kempton.

THIRD SET.

203 Ps. cvi. *v.* 1 *to* 5 : *and* 46 *to end.*   Or **204 (c)** Ps. cvi. *v.* 1 *to* 5 : *and* 46 *to end,*

W. Savage.   *The small notes for* **G. P.** *only.*

204 (a). *v.* 6 *to* 12 : 39 *to* 42 : 45 :   **204 (b)** *v.* 13 *to* 27 : 34 *to* 38 :

Sir G. A. Macfarren.

204 (c) *v.* 28 *to* 33 :   **204 (d).** *v.* 43, 44 :

Day 22.—Morning.

FIRST SET.

115 (a). Venite, *v.* 1 *to* 7 : *and* G. P.

E. G. MONK.

115 (c). *v.* 8 *to* 11 :

205 (a). Ps. cvii. *v.* 1 *to* 3 : 33 *to* 41 :

WALTER MACFARREN.

205 (b). *v.* 4 *to* 7 : 10 *to* 14 : 17 *to* 20 : 28 *to* 30 :

206. *v.* 8, 9 : 15, 16 : 21, 22 : 31, 32 : *and* G. P.

Rev. Sir F. OUSELEY.

205 (c). *v.* 23 *to* 27 :

205 (d). *v.* 42, 43 :

(39)

Day 22.—Morning.

────SECOND SET.────

207 (a).   Venite, *v. 1 to 7 : and G. P.*

Sir R. P. STEWART.

207 (b).   *v. 8 to 11 :*

208 (a).   Ps. cvii. *v. 1 to 3 : and 42 to end.*

J. TURLE.

208 (b).   *v. 4 to 7 : 10 to 14 : 17 to 20 :*

209.   *v. 8, 9 : 15, 16 : 21, 22 : 31, 32 : and G. P.*

J. BATTISHILL.

Or **208 (c).**   *v. 8, 9 : 15, 16 : 21, 22 : 31, 32 : and G. P.*

208 (d).   *v. 23, 24 : 28 : 30 :*

208 (e).   *v. 25 to 27 :*

208 (f).   *v. 29 :*

Slower.

208 (g).   *v. 33 to 41 :*

Or **208 (h).**   G. P. *(ad lib.).*

210 (*a*).   Ps. cviii. *v.* 1 *to* 6 : *and* 10 *to end.*

210 (*b*).   *v.* 7 *to* 9 :

Dr. B. Cooke.

Or 211 (*a*).   Ps. cviii. *v.* 1 *to* 6 : *and* 10 *to end.*

211 (*b*).   *v.* 7 *to* 9 :

Rev. Sir F. Ouseley.

212 (*a*).   Ps. cix. *v.* 1 *to* 4 : 19 *to* 28 :

213 (*a*).   *v.* 5 *to* 18 :

A. B.

Dr. Chard.

212 (*b*).   *v.* 29 *to end.*

Or 213 (*a*).   Ps. cix. *v.* 1 *to* 4 : 19 *to* 28 :

213 (*b*).   *v.* 5 *to* 18 :

Dr. Chard.

213 (*c*).   *v.* 29, 30 :

213 (*d*).   G. P.

Day 23.—Morning.

86 (a).   Venite, *v. 1 to 7 : and G. P.*

86 (b).   *v. 8 to 11 :*

From W. BYRDE.

214 (a).   Ps. cx. *v. 1, 2 : and 5 to end.*

214 (b).   *v. 3, 4 :*

Rev. Sir F. OUSELEY.

215 (a).   Ps. cxi. *v. 1 to 8 : and G. P.*

215 (b).   *v. 9, 10 :*

Dr. C. STEGGALL.

216 (a).   Ps. cxii. *v. 1 to 9 : and G. P.*

216 (b).   *v. 10 :*

Sir G. A. MACFARREN.

217 (a).   Ps. cxiii. *v. 1 to 5 : and G. P.*

217 (b).   *v. 6 to 8 :*

Sir R. P. STEWART.

Or 218 (a).   Ps. cxiii. *v. 1 to 5 : and G. P.*

218 (b).   *v. 6 to 8 :*

E. G. MONK.

Day 23.—Evening.

———— FIRST SET. ————

219 (a).   Ps. cxiv. *v.* 1 *to* 6 : *and* G. P.

Dr. W. HAYES.

219 (b).   *v.* 7, 8 :

220 (a).   Ps. cxv. *v.* 1 *to* 8 : *and* 12 *to end.*

Sir G. A. MACFARREN.

220 (b).   *v.* 9 *to* 11 :

———— SECOND SET. ————

221 (a).   Ps. cxiv. *v.* 1 *to* 6 : *and* G. P.

Ancient.

221 (b).   *v.* 7, 8 :

222 (a).   Ps. cxv. *v.* 1 *to* 8 : *and* 12 *to end.*

Ancient.   Har. by Dr. E. J. HOPKINS.

222 (b).   *v.* 9 *to* 11 :

(43)

Day 24.—Morning.

223 (a).   Venite, *v.* 1 *to* 7 : *and* G. P.

Sir G. A. Macfarren.

223 (b).   *v.* 8 *to* 11 :

224 (a).   Ps. cxvi. *v.* 1 *to* 10 : *and* 14 *to end.*

E. G. Monk.

224 (b).   *v.* 11 *to* 13 :

225.   Ps. cxvii.

Rev. Sir F. Ouseley.

226.   Ps. cxviii. *v.* 1 *to* 4 : *and* 19 *to end.*

Rev. W. H. Havergal.

227 (a).   *v.* 5 *to* 9 ; 15 *to* 18 :

F. A. G. O.

227 (b).   *v.* 10 *to* 14 :

Or, without change of Melody, 227 (a) *v.* 1 *to* 9 : *and* 19 *to end* : 227 (b) *v.* 10 *to* 18 :

Or **228 (a).**   Ps. cxviii. *v.* 1 *to* 9 : *and* 19 *to end.*

J. Turle.

228 (b).   *v.* 10 *to* 18 :

Day 24.—Evening.

229.   Ps. cxix. *v.* 1 *to* 8 : *and* G. P.

Rev. T. Helmore.

Or **230.**   *v.* 1 *to* 8 : *and* G. P.

Henry T. Monk.

231.   *v.* 9 *to* 16 : *and* G. P.

Matthew Camidge.

232.   *v.* 17 *to* 24 : *and* G. P.

From Dr. P. Hayes.

233.   *v.* 25 *to* 32 : *and* G. P.

Sir G. A. Macfarren.

Or **234.**   *v.* 25 *to* 32 : *and* G. P.

Sir G. J. Elvey.

(45)

Day 25.—Morning.

75 (a).   Venite, *v.* 1 *to* 7 : *and* G. P.

75 (b).   *v.* 8 *to* 11 :

W. Bower.

235.   Ps. cxix. *v.* 33 *to* 40 : *and* G. P.

236.   *v.* 41 *to* 48 : *and* G. P.

Dr. L. Colborne.

J. Travers.

237.   *v.* 49 *to* 56 : *and* G. P.

238.   *v.* 57 *to* 64 : *and* G. P.

Old Scotch Chant.

K. J. Pye.

239.   *v.* 65 *to* 72 : *and* G. P.

Sir J. Goss.

Day 25.—Evening.

240.   Ps. cxix. *v.* 73 *to* 80 : *and* G. P.

241.   *v.* 81 *to* 88 : *and* G. P.

Dr. J. Alcock.

Dr. T. Aylward.

242.   *v.* 89 *to* 96 : *and* G. P.

243.   *v.* 97 *to* 104 : *and* G. P.

Sir G. A. Macfarren.

E. G. Monk

Day 26.—Morning.

244 (a). Venite, v. 1 to 7: and G. P.

244 (b). v. 8 to 11:

From TOMLINSON.

245. Ps. cxix. v. 105 to 112: and G. P.

Uncertain.

246. v. 113 to 120: and G. P.

W. H. GARLAND.

247. v. 121 to 128: and G. P.

Sir G. J. ELVEY.

248. v. 129 to 136: and G. P.

ADAPTED.

249. v. 137 to 144: and G. P.

A. H. BROWN.

Day 26.—Evening.

250. Ps. cxix. v. 145 to 152: and G. P.

REV. Sir F. OUSELEY.

251. v. 153 to 160: and G. P.

E. G. MONK.

252. v. 161 to 168: and G. P.

REV. W. H. HAVERGAL.

253. v. 169 to 176: and G. P.

Sir G. J. ELVEY

254 (a).   Venite, *v.* 1 *to* 7 : *and* G. P.

254 (b).   *v.* 8 *to* 11 :

J. Hindle.

255 (a).   Ps. cxx. *v.* 1 *to* 3 : *and* G. P.

255 (b).   *v.* 4 *to* 6 :

Dr. T. S. Dupuis.

256 (a).   Ps. cxxi. *v.* 1 *to* 4 : *and* 7 *to end.*

256 (b).   *v.* 5, 6 :

From Dupuis.

257 (a).   Ps. cxxii. *v.* 1 *to* 5 : *and* 8 *to end.*

257 (b).   *v.* 6, 7 :

Sir G. A. Macfarren.

258 (a).   Ps. cxxiii. *v.* 1, 2 : *and* G. P.

258 (b).   *v.* 3, 4 :

From W. Dyce.

259 (a).   Ps. cxxiv. *v.* 1, 2 : *and* 5 *to end.*

259 (b).   *v.* 3, 4 :

C. King.

260 (a).   cxxv. *v.* 1 *to* 3 : *and* G. P.

260 (b).   *v.* 4, 5 :

Dr. E. J. Hopkins.

Day 27.—Evening.

261 (a).   Ps. cxxvi. *v. 1 to 4 : and G. P.*   261 (b).   *v. 5 to 7 :*

J. DATTISHILL.

262 (a).   Ps. cxxvii. *v. 1 to 3 : and G. P.*   262 (b).   *v. 4 to 6 :*

Right Rev. Bishop TURTON.

263 (a).   Ps. cxxviii. *v. 1 to 4 : and G. P.*   263 (b).   *v. 5 to 7 :*

E. PROUT.

264 (a).   Ps. cxxix. *v. 1 to 4 : and G. P.*   264 (b).   *v. 5 to 8 :*

Sir G. A. MACFARREN.

265 (a).   Ps. cxxx. *v. 1 to 4 : and G. P.*   265 (b).   *v. 5 to 8 :*

E. G. MONK.

266 (a).   Ps. cxxxi. *v. 1 to 2 : and 4 to end.*   266 (b).   *v. 3 :*

J. TURLE.

(49)

Day 28.—Morning.

98 (a).   Venite, *v. 1 to 7 : and G. P.*

Sir G. A. MACFARREN.

98 (b).   *v. 8 to 11 :*

267 (a). Ps. cxxxii. *v. 1 to 7 : 11 to 17 : and G. P.*

Anonymous.

267 (b).   *v. 8 to 10 : 18, 19 :*

268.   Ps. cxxxiii.

E. G. MONK.

269.   Ps. cxxxiv.

G. H. E. MASSY DAWSON.

270.   Ps. cxxxv. *v. 1 to 4 : and 19 to end.*

Dr. C. STEGGALL.

271 (a).   *v. 5 to 18 :*

R. H. STANLEY.

Or { **271 (a).**   *v. 1 to 14 : and 19 to end.*
{ **271 (b).**   *v. 15 to 18 :*

---FIRST SET.---

272 (a). **Ps. cxxxvi.** *v.* 1 *to* 9 : **16** *to* 22 : *and* G. P.

T. Purcell.

272 (b). *v.* 10 *to* 15 :

272 (c). *v.* 23 *to* 25 :

272 (d). *v.* 26, 27 :

272 (e). G. P. (*ad lib.*).

273 (a). **Ps. cxxxvii.** *v.* 1 *to* 3 : *and* 7 *to end.*

273 (b). *v.* 4 *to* 6 :

H. Purcell.

274 (a). **Ps. cxxxviii.** *v.* 1 *to* 6 : *and* G. P.

274 (b). *v.* 7, 8 :

F. Champneys.

(51)

Day 28.—Evening.

SECOND SET.

275 (a). **Ps. cxxxvi.** *v.* 1 *to* 9 : 16 *to* 22 : *and* 26 *to end.*

J. Turle.

275 (b). *v.* 10 *to* 15 :

275 (c). *v.* 23 *to* 25 :

276 (a). **Ps. cxxxvii.** *v.* 1 *to* 3 : *and* 7 *to end.*

From Dupuis.

276 (b). *v.* 4 *to* 6 ;

277 (a). **Ps. cxxxviii.** *v.* 1 *to* 6 : *and* G. P.

Dr. Mark J. Monk.

277 (b). *v.* 7, 8 :

Or 278 (a). **Ps. cxxxviii.** *v.* 1 *to* 6 : *and* G. P.

Hackett.

278 (b). *v.* 7, 8 :

189 (a).   Venite, *v.* 1 *to* 7 : *and* G. P.

189 (b).   *v.* 8 *to* 11 :

Anonymous.

279 (a).   **Ps. cxxxix.** *v.* 1 *to* 18 : *and* 23 *to end.*

Dr. M. Green.

279 (b).   *v.* 19 *to* 22 :

279 (c).   G. P. (*ad lib.*).

280 (a).   **Ps. clx.** *v.* 1 *to* 5 : *and* 12 *to end.*

280 (b).   *v.* 6 *to* 11 :

E. G. Monk.

281 (a).   **Ps. cxli.** *v.* 1 *to* 4 : *and* 9 *to end.*

281 (b).   *v.* 5 *to* 8 :

Rev. Sir F. Ouseley.

FIRST SET.

282 (a). Ps. cxlii. v. 1 to 5: and G. P.

282 (b). v. 6 to 9:

Dr. T. S. Dupuis.

283 (a). Ps. cxliii. v. 1 to 6: and G. P.

283 (b). v. 7 to 12:

Sir G. A. Macfarren.

SECOND SET.

284 (a). Ps. cxlii. v. 1 to 5: and G. P.

284 (b). v. 6 to 9:

C. King.

285 (a). Ps. cxliii. v. 1 to 6: and G. P.

285 (b). v. 7 to 12:

A. H. Littleton.

Day 30.—Morning.

56 (a). Venite, v. 1 to 7 ; and G. P.

56 (b). v. 8 to 11 :

Dr. W. Hayes.

286 (a). Ps. cxliv. v. 1 to 4 : 9 to 11 : and G. P.

J. Battishill.

286 (b). v. 5 to 8 :

286 (c). v. 12 to 15 :

287 (a). Ps. cxlv. v. 1 to 7 : and 14 to end.

287 (b). v. 8 to 13 :

Dr. H. Aldrich.

288 (a). Ps. cxlvi. v. 1 to 6 : and 10 to end.

288 (b). v. 7 to 9 :

Dr. Armes.

Or 289 (a). Ps. cxlvi. v. 1 to 6 : and 10 to end.

289 (b). v. 7 to 9 :

Dr. J. Clarke-Whitfield.

(55)

290 (*a*).   **Ps. cxlvii.** *v.* 1 *to* 7 : *and* 12 *to end.*

290 (*b*).   *v.* 8 *to* 11 :

From Rev. W. FELTON.

291 (*a*).   **Ps. cxlviii.** *v.* 1 *to* 6 ; *and* 13 *to end.*

291 (*b*).   *v.* 7 *to* 12 :

TOMLINSON.

292 (*a*).   **Ps. clxix.** *v.* 1 *to* 4 : *and* G. P.

292 (*b*).   *v.* 5 *to* 9 :

Rev. Sir F. OUSELEY.

293 (*a*).   **Ps. cl.** *v.* 1, 2 : *and* 6 *to end.*

293 (*b*).   *v.* 3 *to* 5 :

Sir G. J. ELVEY.

Day 31.—Morning.

294 (a).   Venite, *v.* 1 *to* 7 : *and* G. P.

P. FUSSELL.

294 (b).   *v.* 8 *to* 11 :

295 (a).   Ps. cxliv. *v.* 1 *to* 4 : 9 *to* 11 : *and* G. P.

HARVEY LÖHR.

295 (b).   *v.* 5 *to* 8 :

295 (c).   *v.* 12 *to* 15 :

296 (a). ' Ps. cxlv. *v.* 1 *to* 7 : *and* 14 *to end.*

E. G. MONK.

296 (b).   *v.* 8 *to* 13 :

297 (a).   Ps. cxlvi. *v.* 1 *to* 6 : *and* 10 *to end.*

DR. R. WOODWARD.

297 (b).   *v.* 7 *to* 9 :

Or **298 (a).** Ps. cxlvi. *v.* 1 *to* 6 : *and* 10 *to end.*

REV. W. H. HAVERGAL.

298 (b)   *v.* 7 *to* 9 :

Or **299.**   Ps. cxlvi.

On an Ancient C. F,

Day 31.—Evening.

300 (*a*).   Ps. cxlvii. *v.* 1 *to* 7 : *and* 12 *to end.*

300 (*b*).   *v.* 8 *to* 11 :

Ancient. Har. by Dr. GARRETT.

301 (*a*).   Ps. cxlviii. *v.* 1 *to* 6 : *and* 13 *to end.*

301 (*b*).   *v.* 7 *to* 12 :

H. BAKER.

302 (*a*).   Ps. cxlix. *v.* 1 *to* 4 : *and* G. P.

302 (*b*).   *v.* 5 *to* 9 :

Rev. Sir F. OUSELEY.

303.   Ps. cl.

Sir G. J. ELVEY.

Or 304 (*a*). Ps. cl. *v.* 1, 2 : *and* 6 *to end.*

304 (*b*).   *v.* 3 *to* 5 :

Dr. MARK J. MONK

(58)

PROPER PSALMS ON CERTAIN DAYS.

Christmas Day.—Morning.

13 (a).   Venite, *v. 1 to 7 : and* G. P.

Dr. T. A. WALMISLEY.

13 (b).   *v. 8 to 11 :*

33 (a).   Ps. xix. *v. 1 to 11 : and 15 to end.*

From J. BATTISHILL.

33 (b).   *v. 12 to 14 :*

90 (a).   Ps. xlv. *v. 1 to 10 : and 17 to end.*

W. LEE.

90 (b).   *v. 11 to 16 :*

160 (a).   Ps. lxxxv. *v. 1 to 3 : and 8 to end.*

Dr. W. CROTCH.

160 (b).   *v. 4 to 7 :*

Or **161 (a).**   Ps. lxxxv. *v. 1 to 3 : and 8 to end.*

E. G. MONK.

161 (b).   *v. 4 to 7 :*

168 (a).   Ps. lxxxix. v. 1 *to* 4 : 16 *to* 19 :

168 (b).   v. 5 to 15 :

Dr. W. Hayes.

169 (a).   v. 20 *to* 30 : 33 *to* 36 :

169 (b).   v. 31, 32.

W. Dyce.

170 (a).   v. 37 *to* 44 : 49 :

170 (b).   v. 45 *to* 48 :

Sir G. A. Macfarren.

170 (c).   v. 50 :

168 (a).   G. P.

f slower.

Or, Ps. lxxxix. to one Melody, throughout, as in the following page.

214 (a).   Ps. cx. v. 1, 2 : *and* 5 *to end.*

214 (b).   v. 3, 4 :

Tr.

Rev. Sir F. Ouseley.

267 (a).   Ps. cxxxii. v. 1 *to* 7 : 11 *to* 17 ; *and* G. P.

267 (b).   v. 8 *to* 10 : 18, 19 :

Anonymous.

(60)

Christmas Day.—Evening (continued).

168 (a). Ps. lxxxix. v. 1 to 19 : 33 to 36 : and G. P.

Tr.

Dr. W. Hayes.

168 (b). v. 20 to 32 :

168 (c). v. 37 to 44 : 49 :

168 (d). r. 45 to 48 :

168 (e). v. 50 :

f Slower.

168 (f). G. P. (ad lib.)

214 (a). Ps. cx. v. 1, 2 : and 5 to end.

Tr.

Rev. Sir F. Ouseley.

214 (b). v. 3, 4 :

267 (a). Ps. cxxxii. v. 1 to 7 : 11 to 17 : and G. P.

Tr.

Anonymous.

267 (b). v. 8 to 10 : 18, 19 :

Ash Wednesday.—Morning.

———FIRST SET.———

134 (a). Venite, v. 1 to 7 : and G. P.

Tr.

Dr. W. Crotch.

134 (b). v. 8 to 11 :

7 (a). Ps. vi. 1 to 7 : and G. P.

Tr.

E. G. Monk.

7 (b). v. 8 to 10 :

61 (a). Ps. xxxii. v. 1, 2 : and 7 to end.

Dr. Dunnett.

61 (b). v. 3 to 6 :

76 (a). Ps. xxxviii. v. 1 to 10 : and 15 to end.

R. Farrant.

76 (b). v. 11 to 14 :

(62)

Ash Wednesday.—Morning (continued).

————SECOND SET.————

64 (a). Venite, *v. 1 to 7 : and* G. P.

T. TALLIS.

64 (b). *v. 8 to 11 :*

10 (a). Ps. vi. *v. 1 to 7 : and* G. P.

Sir J. GOSS.

10 (b). *v. 8 to 10 :*

60 (a). Ps. xxxii. *v. 1, 2 : and 7 to end.*

Tr.

E. G. MONK.

60 (b). *v. 3 to 6 :*

77 (a). Ps. xxxviii. *v. 1 to 10 : and 15 to end.*

Tr.

T. KELWAY.

77 (b). *v. 11 to 14 :*

(63)

Ash Wednesday.—Evening.

190   Ps. cii. *v.* 1 *to* 11 : *and* 23 *to end.*

Or, 190 throughout Ps. cii.   Dr. W. Crotch.

191.   *v.* 12 *to* 22 :   Or 192   *v.* 23 *to end.*

Major.

E. G. M.   Dr. W. Crotch.

265 (*a*).   Ps. cxxx. *v.* 1 *to* 4 : *and* G. P.

E. G. Monk.

265 (*b*).   *v.* 5 *to* 8 :

285 (*a*).   Ps. cxliii. *v.* 1 *to* 6 : *and* G. P.

A. H. Littleton.

285 (*b*).   *v.* 7 *to* 12 :

(64)

Good Friday.—Morning.

32 (a).   Venite, v. 1 to 7 : and G. P.

Rev. W. Tucker.

32 (b).   v. 8 to 11 :

41 (a).   Ps. xxii. v. 1 to 21 : and G. P.

Tr.

Dr. J. Blow.

42.   v. 22 to end.

Tr.

Rev. W. H. Havergal.

Or 41 (b).   v. 22 to 32 :

79 (a).   Ps. xl. v. 1 to 13 : and 19 to end.

Tr.

E. Frost.

79 (b).   v. 14 to 18 :

105 (a).   Ps. liv. v. 1 to 3 : and 6 to end.

Tr.

J. T. Cooper.

105 (b).   v. 4, 5 :

Good Friday.—Evening.

128 (a).   Ps. lxix. *v.* 1 *to* 12 : 20 *to* 29 :

T. TALLIS.

128 (b).   *v.* 13 *to* 19 :

129.   *v.* 30 *to end.*   **Or 128 (c).**   *v.* 30 *to end.*

E. G. MONK.

167 (a).   Ps. lxxxviii. *v.* 1 *to* 9 : *and* 13 *to end.*

Tr.

E. G. M.

167 (b).   *v.* 10 *to* 12 :

Easter Day.—Morning.

254 (a). Anthems, *v.* 1, 2: *and 6 to end.*

254 (b). *v.* 3 *to* 5:

J. HINDLE.

Or 9 (a). Anthems, *v.* 1, 2: *and 6 to end.*

9 (b). *v.* 3 *to* 5:

P. HUMPHREYS.

Or 305 (a). Anthems, *v.* 1, 2: *and 6 to end.*

305 (b). *v.* 3 *to* 5:

E. G. M.

3 (a). Ps. ii. *v.* 1 *to* 3: *and* G. P.

3 (b). *v.* 4 *to* 6:

E. G. MONK.

3 (c). *v.* 7 *to* 9:

3 (d). *v.* 10 *to* 12:

110 (b). Ps. lvii. *v.* 1 *to* 5:

110 (a). *v.* 6 *to end:*

E. J. BELLERBY.

215 (a). Ps. cxi. *v.* 1 *to* 8: *and* G. P.

215 (b). *v.* 9, 10:

Dr. C. STEGGALL.

Easter Day.—Evening.

————FIRST SET.————

217 (a).   **Ps. cxiii.** *v. 1 to 5 : and G. P.*

Sir R. P. Stewart.

217 (b).   *v. 6 to 8 :·*

221 (a).   **Ps. cxiv.** *v. 1 to 6 : and G. P.*

Ancient.

221 (b).   *v. 7, 8 :*

228 (a).   **Ps. cxviii.** *v. 1 to 9 : and 19 to end.*

J. Turle.

228 (b).   *v. 10 to 18 :*

————SECOND SET.————

218 (a).   **Ps. cxiii.** *v. 1 to 5 : and G. P.*

E. G. Monk.

218 (b).   *v. 6 to 8 :*

219 (a).   **Ps. cxiv.** *v. 1 to 6 : and G. P.*

Dr. W. Hayes.

219 (b).   *v. 7, 8 :*

227 (a).   **Ps. cxviii.** *v. 1 to 9 : and 19 to end.*

Rev. Sir F. Ouseley.

227 (b).   *v. 10 to 18 :*

Ascension Day.—Morning.

———FIRST SET.———

294 (a). Venite, *v. 1 to 7 : and G. P.*

P. FUSSELL.

294 (b). *v. 8 to 11 :*

9 (a). Ps. viii. *v. 1 to 3 : and 9 to end.*

P. HUMPHREYS.

9 (b). *v. 4 to 8 :*

21 (a). Ps. xv. *v. 1, 2 : and 7 to end.*

Rev. Dr. DYKES.

21 (b). *v. 3 to 6 :*

35 (a). Ps. xxi. *v. 1 to 7 : and 13 to end.*

Dr. T. S. DUPUIS.

35 (b). *v. 8 to 12 :*

Or **36 (a).** Ps. xxi. *v. 1 to 7 : and 13 to end.*

Rev. W. H. HAVERGAL.

36 (b). *v. 8 to 12 :*

(69)

F

————SECOND SET.————

180 (a).   Venite, *v.* 1 *to* 7 : *and* G. P.   **180 (b).**   *v.* 8 *o* 11 :

Ancient.

12 (a).   Ps. viii. *v.* 1 *to* 3 : *and* 9 *to end.*   **12 (b).**   *v.* 4 *to* 8 :

Dr. E. J. HOPKINS.

26 (a).   Ps. xv. *v.* 1, 2 : *and* 7 *to end.*   **26 (b).**   *v.* 3 *to* 6 :

Rev. T. R. MATTHEWS

40 (a).   Ps. xxi. *v.* 1 *to* 7 : *and* 13 *to end.*   **40 (b).**   *v.* 8 *to* 12 :

E. G. MONK.

Ascension Day.—Evening.

49 (a).   Ps. XXIV. *v.* 1 *to* 6 :

Tr.

Dr. S. Arnold.

49 (b).   *v.* 7 : 9 : *and* G. P.

49 (c).   *v.* 8 : 10 :

TREBLES ONLY.   FULL.

* If sung by Men only, or Full, play Bass (* *) 8ve lower.

92 (a).   Ps. XLVII. *v.* 1 *to* 4 : *and* 8 *to end.*

Dr. E. Ayrton.

92 (b).   *v.* 5 *to* 7 :

211 (a).   Ps. CVIII. *v.* 1 *to* 6 : *and* 10 *to end.*

Rev. Sir F. Ouseley.

211 (b).   *v.* 7 *to* 9 :

Whitsunday.—Morning.

134 (a).   Venite, *v.* 1 *to* 7 : *and* G. P.

Dr. W. Crotch.

134 (b).   *v.* 8 *to* 11 :

96 (a).   Ps. xlviii. *v.* 1, 2 : *and* 8 *to end.*

E. G. Monk.

96 (b).   *v.* 3 *to* 7 :

125.   Ps. lxviii. *v.* 1 *to* 6 : *and* 19 *to* 23 :

From W. Russell.

126 (a).   *v.* 7 *to* 14 : 24 *to* 31 : *and* G. P.

Dr. E. F. Rimbault.

126 (b).   *v.* 15 *to* 18 : 32 *to* 35 :

Or **126 (a).** Ps. lxviii. *v.* 1 *to* 18 : 24 *to* 31 : *and* G. P.

Dr. E. F. Rimbault.

126 (c).   *v.* 19 *to* 23 :

126 (b).   *v.* 32 *to* 35 :

Whitsunday.—Evening.

———— FIRST SET. ————

195 (a). Ps. civ. *v.* 1 *to* 4 : 24 *to* 30 : *and* 33 *to end.*

195 (b). *v.* 5 *to* 10 :

Rev. Sir F. Ouseley.

196 (a). *v.* 11 *to* 18 : 23 :

196 (b). *v.* 19 *to* 22 :

B. Lamb.

195 (c). *v.* 31, 32 :

296 (a). Ps. cxlv. *v.* 1 *to* 7 : *and* 14 *to end.*

296 (b). *v.* 8 *to* 13 :

E. G. Monk.

196 (a).   Ps. civ. v. 1 to 4 : 24 to 30 : and G. P.

Tr.

B. LAMB.

196 (c).   v. 5 to 10 : 19 to 23 : 31 to 35 :

196 (d).   v. 11 to 18 :

287 (a).   Ps. cxlv. v. 1 to 7 : and 14 to end.

Dr. H. ALDRICH.

287 (b).   v. 8 to 13 :

Solemnization of Matrimony.

263 (a).   Ps. cxxviii. *v.* 1 *to* 4 : *and* G. P.

263 (b).   *v.* 5 *to* 7 :

E. PROUT.

123 (a).   *Or* Ps. lxvii. *v.* 1, 2 : 4 : 6, 7 :

123 (b).   *v.* 3 : 5 : *and* G. P.

Dr. C. STEGGALL.

Visitation of the Sick.

135 (a).   Ps. lxxi. *v.* 1 *to* 5 : *and* 12 *to end.*

135 (b).   *v.* 6 *to* 11 :

Dr. C. GIBBONS.

Burial of the Dead.

78 (a).   Ps. xxxix. *v.* 1 *to* 4 : 8 *to* 12 : *and* G. P.

78 (b).   *v.* 5 *to* 7 : 13 *to* 15 :

Rev. W. FELTON.

172 (a).   *Or* Ps. xc. *v.* 1 *to* 6 : *and* 13 *to end.*

172 (b).   *v.* 7 *to* 12 :

Dr. W. CROFT.

Churching of Women.

224 (a). Ps. cxvi. *v. 1 to 10 : and 14 to end.*

E. G. Monk.

224 (b). *v. 11 to 13 :*

262 (a). *Or* Ps. cxxvii. *v. 1 to 3 : and* G. P.

Right Rev. Bishop Turton.

262 (b). *v. 4 to 6 :*

Commination.

102 (a). Ps. li. *v. 1 to 13 : and 18 to end.*

From J. Goldwin.

102 (b). *v. 14 to 17 :*

At Sea.

THANKSGIVING AFTER A STORM.

———————— FIRST SET. ————————

122 (a). Ps. lxvi. v. 1 to 8 : and 14 to end.

122 (b). v. 9 to 13 :

Dr. T. A. WALMISLEY.

309 (a). Ps. cvii. v. 1 to 3 : 8, 9 : 15, 16 : 21, 22 : 31, 32 : and G. P.

J. TURLE.

309 (b). v. 4 to 7 : 10 to 14 : 17 to 20 : 33 to 41 :

309 (c). v. 23 to 28 : 30 :

309 (d). v. 29 :

p Slower.

309 (e). v. 42, 43 :

(77)

At Sea (continued).

————SECOND SET.————

314 (a). Ps. lxvi. *v. 1 to 8 : and 14 to end.*

Ancient.

314 (b). *v. 9 to 13 :*

208 (a). Ps. cvii. *v. 1 to 3 : and 42 to end.*

J. TURLE.

208 (b). *v. 4 to 7 : 10 to 14 : 17 to 20 :*

209. *v. 8, 9 : 15, 16 : 21, 22 : 31, 32 : and G. P.*

J. BATTISHILL.

Or **208 (c).** *v. 8, 9 : 15, 16 : 21, 22 : 31, 32 : and G. P.*

208 (d). *v. 23, 24 : 28 : 30 :*

208 (e). *v. 25 to 27 :*

208 (f). *v. 29 :*

Slower.

208 (g). *v. 33 to 41 :*

Or **208 (h).** G. P. (*ad lib.*).

AN HYMN OF PRAISE AND THANKSGIVING AFTER A DANGEROUS TEMPEST.

315 (*a*).   *v. 1 to 5 : and 13 to end.*

Rev. Sir F. Ouseley.

315 (*b*).   *v. 6 to 12 :*

AFTER VICTORY OR DELIVERANCE FROM AN ENEMY.

318 (*a*).   *v. 1 to 5 : and 9 to end.*

York Processional.

318 (*b*).   *v. 6 to 8 :*

(79)

Queen's Accession.

Hymn instead of " Venite."

20 (a).   *v.* 1 *to* 4 : *and* 11 *to end.*

From R. Goodson.

20 (b).   *v.* 5 *to* 10 :

Or 115 (a).   *v.* 1 *to* 4 : *and* 11 *to end.*

E. G. Monk.

115 (b).   *v* 5 *to* 10 :

34 (a).   Ps. xx. *v.* 1 *to* 5 : 7, 8 : *and* G. P.

J. Travers.

34 (b).   *v.* 6 : 9 :

35 (a).   Ps. xxi. *v.* 1 *to* 7 : *and* 13 *to end.*

Dr. T. S. Dupuis.

35 (b).   *v.* 8 *to* 12 :

187.   Ps. ci.

Taylor.

(80)

Additional Chants for "Venite."

306.

Rev. W. H. Havergal.

307.

R. H. Stevenson.

308.

Rev. Sir F. Ouseley.

309.

J. Turle.

310.

A. H. Brown.

Appendix.

311.

T. Purcell.

312.

Rev. Dr. H. Aldrich.

313.

Ancient.

314.

Ancient.

315.

Rev. Sir F. Ouseley.

316.

F. A. G. O.

317.

E. G. Monk.

318.

York Processional.

www.ingramcontent.com/pod-product-compliance
Lightning Source LLC
Chambersburg PA
CBHW032249080426
42735CB00008B/1061

* 9 7 8 3 3 3 7 2 9 6 8 9 6 *